YOUR ART, GOD'S HEART:
A 21 Day Devotional for Creatives

Allen C. Paul

Copyright © 2018 by Allen C. Paul

All rights reserved. This book or any portion thereof may not be reproduced or used in any manner whatsoever without the express written permission of the publisher except for the use of brief quotations in a book review.

Printed in the United States of America

First Printing, 2018

ISBN 978-0-9972703-5-8

www.GodandGigs.com

All Scripture quotations, unless otherwise indicated, are taken from the Holy Bible, New International Version®, NIV®. Copyright ©1973, 1978, 1984, 2011 by Biblica, Inc.™ Used by permission of Zondervan. All rights reserved worldwide. www.zondervan.com The "NIV" and "New International Version" are trademarks registered in the United States Patent and Trademark Office by Biblica, Inc.™

Scripture quotations marked NKJV are taken from the New King James Version®. Copyright © 1982 by Thomas Nelson. Used by permission. All rights reserved.

Scripture quotations marked NASB are taken from the NEW AMERICAN STANDARD BIBLE(R), Copyright (C) 1960,1962,1963,1968,1971,1972,1973,1975,1977,1995 by The Lockman Foundation. Used by permission.

DEVOTIONAL SCHEDULE AND CONTENTS

INTRODUCTION 5
Days 1- 4 7
    DAY 1 8
    DAY 2 10
    DAY 3 12
    DAY 4 14
Days 5-6 17
    DAY 5 18
    DAY 6 20
Days 7-8 22
    DAY 7 23
    DAY 8 25
DAYS 9-11 27
    DAY 9 28
    DAY 10 31
    DAY 11 33
DAYS 12-14 35
    DAY 12 36
    DAY 13 39
    DAY 14 42
DAYS 15-17 45
    DAY 15 46
    DAY 16 49
    DAY 17 52
DAYS 18-21 55
    DAY 18 56

DAY 19 58
DAY 20 61
DAY 21 64
Additional Resources from God and Gigs 67

INTRODUCTION

It's not easy, I know.

Whether you are a creative professional, or just someone who loves the arts, you've probably found yourself feeling low and uninspired at times. The creative act by its very nature pulls a lot out of us. Thankfully, there is a way to find consistent renewal and purpose in our creative calling.

The key? It's connecting with our Creator.

For the faith-focused artist, no amount of rehearsal, career counseling, networking or education can substitute for a personal relationship with God. We'll always find ourselves lacking in inspiration if we don't prioritize spiritual development. In my humble opinion, the best way to develop spiritually is to practice daily routines of prayer and Bible study. That's why I wrote this devotional guide for you– because sometimes we need a little structure to help us get spiritually organized.

This devotional guide is written as a companion to my guide for musicians, "God and Gigs: Succeed as a Musician without Sacrificing your Faith," but it can be used anytime you need a daily reminder of God's heart for you as an artist. Each devotional consists of a short reading, a prayer and a Scripture to read and meditate on throughout the day. The entire reading may only take minutes of your day, but the power is in the consistent application of the principles. Each day, make sure to find a way to act on the principle you have prayed and thought about as you go about your creative activities. It's this process that will deepen your spiritual understanding of your artistic abilities.

I encourage you to keep a journal alongside your devotional reading, so that the moments you spend thinking and praying are captured in physical form. Something about writing down what you are thinking about makes it easier to apply to your life.

I pray you'll be refreshed and reinvigorated as you go through this 21 day journey, and that as you connect more deeply with God's heart, he'll in turn bless your art.

Gratefully, Allen C. Paul

Days 1- 4
Stay Connected

DAY 1

Where are you?

Imagine you are Adam or Eve, the first people ever created. You're gifted with all the wisdom and creative energy God could possibly provide. Except for one tree God forbids you to eat from, you have the entire world at your disposal. But then you make a mistake – a very costly mistake. What do you do next?

Many of you know what Adam and Eve did after their misstep. They hid from God, who was used to meeting with them face-to-face. When God showed up for their talk, his first question to them wasn't about whether Adam had been productive that day in his gardening or whether Eve had worked hard enough to keep the animals in check. He asked, "Where are you?" While their physical location hadn't changed, their spiritual position had shifted. Clearly, Adam and Eve's choice moved them in a direction they would regret.

We can't begin a journey unless we know our current location. Every step toward spiritual and lifelong success begins with an honest assessment of where we currently are. As creative beings, we are often good at seeing the truth in others, but not always in ourselves. We can obscure our self-image with excuses, by hiding behind more work and projects, or by ignoring the signs of burnout and depression. But nothing will change until we admit that we need to change.

Today, make a commitment to understand and acknowledge where you really are. You may have to admit that you are in a sad, frustrated, or lonely place. Don't let that stop you from starting the journey. God can take you from where you are to where you are supposed to be if you choose to trust him.

Prayer

Lord, I know I can easily lose my way in this creative journey. Traps and detours tend to distract me, and I sometimes choose to hide from the reality that I'm not where I want to be. Today, show me exactly where I am spiritually, and more importantly, guide me to the place where you want me to be. In Jesus' name, amen.

Scripture To Meditate On

Search me, God, and know my heart; test me and know my anxious thoughts. See if there is any offensive way in me, and lead me in the way everlasting.
- Psalms 139:23

ALLEN C. PAUL

DAY 2

Connect With Your True Friends

Being an artist can be a lonely profession. We can spend hours, even days, in seclusion when working on a song or project. Our only conversation might be with ourselves as we toil through chords, lyrics, and lines. And, while we generally work with others to bring a project to life, at the end of the day, we feel a personal connection to the work we create. If it fails to succeed, we feel the weight of failure squarely on our shoulders. But God did not design us to walk this journey alone.

In 1 Samuel 22, David, who was a songwriter and musician as well as a warrior, was hiding from King Saul. Clearly, he was felt he was alone in his fight to stay alive. But when he hides in the cave of Adullum, scripture tells us that both his family and 400 other distressed people – men in debt, on the outside, under pressure – joined him in the cave. It's like they gravitated to someone who understood what it was like to feel alone. That's what our church, and our fellow artists, can do for us.

In order to grow, we must stay in fellowship with those

who understand our story and can be a shoulder to lean on when things get tough. Today, meditate and honestly ask yourself if God has sent people to be your support, both in your ministry and in your artistic circles. If you haven't connected deeply with them, start making those connections right away.

Prayer

Lord, I know that my creativity can lead me into a place of seclusion and disconnection. Sometimes, I hide myself from the people around me, because I assume they don't understand. But I trust that you will never leave me nor forsake me. I know you've placed other people in my life to help me feel your presence and to encourage me to keep going. Help me today to seek out and grow those Godly relationships. Thank you for your ever-present love and influence. In Jesus' name, amen.

Scripture To Meditate On

Let us hold unswervingly to the hope we profess, for he who promised is faithful. And let us consider how we may spur one another on toward love and good deeds, not giving up meeting together, as some are in the habit of doing, but encouraging one another--and all the more as you see the day approaching.
- Hebrews 10:23-25

DAY 3

The Price of Creative Success

Solomon, like his father David, was an artistic soul. He penned proverbs, wrote romantic prose, and oversaw the building of mansions and temples. Clearly, his wisdom allowed him to be extremely creative. However, when it came to controlling his own impulses, he failed terribly.

Rather than being satisfied with what God had given him, he says in Ecclesiastes that he held "nothing back from himself." He chose to fill his life with all the trappings of success, yet he felt unfulfilled internally and lost his spiritual foundations. The end of his reign as king was filled with regret and discord, and his legacy was wiped out within a few generations.

He had it all – riches, wisdom, fame, and success. But he lost what was most important.

As creatives, we have an innate desire to see our work thrive and our art gain notoriety. But if we are not careful, the search for fame, glory, and success can consume us.

If we haven't reached the heights of success, that doesn't mean that we aren't searching for it, and not having riches doesn't mean that we aren't obsessed with it. God knows whether those things will pull us closer to him or tear you away.

Like Solomon, we have been given a lot by God, and we can use it to test our limits or we can make sure to remain connected to God through continuous humility and prayer. Submit every desire, talent, and quest for artistic glory to him first. He's the only one that knows which goals will bring us lasting joy.

Prayer

Lord, you've blessed me with creativity, a rich imagination, natural talent, and a drive to succeed. But if I don't surrender my desires, success might be the very thing that tears me away from you. Remind me to put you first, before my desires, wants, and goals. Then I'll look for the blessings that come from your hand, when I have recommitted my heart. In Jesus' name, amen.

Scripture To Meditate On

But seek ye first the kingdom of God, and His righteousness; and all these things shall be added unto you.
- Matthew 6:33

DAY 4

Who Owns Your Gift?

I've always been jealous of people who play more than one instrument. When I meet musicians who have mastered piano, drums, guitar, bass, and more, I often feel inadequate. I'm proficient on my chosen instrument (piano), but I can barely pluck out a few beginner chords on a guitar. I played other instruments in high school, but I never rose to the level that some of my friends have reached.

I know this feeling of inadequacy is totally emotional and unfounded. These artists, while obviously gifted, worked hard to cultivate the talent they have and spread it across multiple activities and instruments. I never pushed harder to learn other instruments mostly because I was unwilling to step back into the seat of the beginner. It's no one's fault but my own. I used to rationalize by saying that playing piano was my calling, but I know I could have added an instrument or two to my skill set. I'm owning up to the fact that God never stopped me from expanding my musical knowledge.

In the parable of the talents, three servants are given varying amounts of resources to manage and invest. Two servants double their investment through hard work and discipline. The other servant buries his resource in the sand. But that's not the biggest issue.

When the master returns and demands an account of their stewardship, the one servant who hid his gift states a telling phrase at the end of his excuses. "Here, take back what is yours."

In other words, the servant tries to limit the master's ownership to the gift alone. Meanwhile, the owner not only had authority over the gift, but he also had authority over the servant himself. The master owned everything, the field, the servant, the position; everything was in the Master's hand, not just the talent he had lent to the servant.

When you evaluate what you will do with your creative talent, remember the gift isn't yours to do with as you please. Not only does your gift belong to the Master – you do as well. View your creative decisions and efforts with the understanding that God claims you as His own.

Prayer

Father, you've made every effort to show how much you love and care for me – from creating me with unique gifts and abilities to sending Your son to save me from my sins. Help me to see that you are interested in much more than my talents and my art – you're interested in me. Don't allow me to limit myself by shrinking my abilities into the convenient box of my own perspective. Help me grow into everything you would have me to be. In Jesus' name, amen.

Scripture To Meditate On

Therefore, I urge you, brothers and sisters, in view of God's mercy, to offer your bodies as a living sacrifice, holy and pleasing to God--this is your true and proper worship.
- Romans 12:1

Days 5-6
Establish Your Priorities

ALLEN C. PAUL

DAY 5

Finish What's On Your Plate

If you had a mother, grandmother, or aunt who was 'old-school', you likely heard these words at dinner time when you were trying to avoid eating your vegetables: finish what's on your plate. In their eyes, not eating your entire meal meant you weren't getting all the nutrition you needed. They were pushing us to make the right choices, even if we didn't like our broccoli or green beans. While we may have wanted to move on to dessert, there would be no sweet treats until we ate the healthy stuff.

Dietary considerations aside, as creatives, there's a lot on our lifestyle plate. Ideas, projects, family and work responsibilities, marketing and branding ourselves, planning for the future... It can feel like there's no way to finish it all. Our plate is full and we want to push the whole thing away at times, running away from the table.

But there are some things we have to take care of, no matter what – the vegetables of the creative life, so to speak. Dedicating time to prayer and bible study daily. Being a good spouse, family member, and friend. Putting our best into our work so that others are inspired.

At one point in His ministry, Jesus' disciples tried to get him to accept a meal after a day of teaching and preaching. His response? "My food is to do the will of him who sent me and to finish His work" (John 4:34).

Make sure you're taking care of the most important stuff on your plate.

Prayer

Father, you've provided me with a lot of blessings, and therefore, a lot of responsibilities. But I want to make sure that I'm focusing on what you desire for my life, not on the things that don't benefit me in the long run. Help me today to finish the things that matter most and to allow your Spirit to guide my decision making, my connections, and my creative drive. In Jesus' name, amen.

Scripture To Meditate On

Blessed are those who hunger and thirst for righteousness, for they will be filled.
- Matthew 5:6

DAY 6

Excellence Starts Within

Search Google for "how to make it in the _____ industry", and you'll find a million sites promising to give you the keys to success. This isn't meant to say that there isn't value in getting education and advice. Building a unique brand, being able to articulate a vision, connecting with other leaders in your field – all of these tactics are valid. But once you are in the room with an audience, it is what you are on the inside that will determine if you will be remembered or rejected.

The book of Daniel explains how he, along with other young Jewish men who were captured by the Babylonians, was selected to serve in the king's court. They all received the same training, were given the same parameters, and were expected to serve in the same way. But, because Daniel walked closely with God and was intimately acquainted with his purpose, he stood out from his contemporaries. This is evident in Daniel 6:3, "Then this Daniel was preferred above the presidents and princes, because an excellent spirit [was] in him; and the king thought to set him over the whole realm."

The excellent spirit Daniel had wasn't a result of a class, a strategy, or a special seminar. It was something activated within him by his faith and his confidence in who had sent him.

Make sure, as you strive for excellence, that you set a foundation of excellence in your spiritual walk. That can only come from constant connection with God and His Word.

Prayer

Father, you've given me a desire to stand out in my industry. My push to be the best isn't a bad thing – you encourage me to let my light shine in this world. But I realize you are the source of excellence, and only by humbling myself under your authority will I achieve true success. Help me to live out your principles and hide your Word in my heart, so that when I speak, perform, and create, it's your glory that becomes evident. In Jesus' name, amen.

Scripture To Meditate On

But we have this treasure in earthen vessels, that the excellence of the power may be of God and not of us.
- 2 Corinthians 4:7 (NKJV)

ALLEN C. PAUL

Days 7-8
Respect The Business

DAY 7

The Golden Rule of Artists

It was singer and songwriter Van Morrison who was quoted as saying, "Music is spiritual. The music business is not." If you've spent any time in the entertainment industry, it's hard to disagree with him. There's very little spirituality and love shown in an industry that seems to reward people who are always looking for an edge over their fellow artists. With so many creative people vying for attention, it seems the only way to be noticed is to climb over the people in front of you. Being aggressive and competitive may be a good business strategy in the short run, but it's a bad choice spiritually.

During Jesus' earthly ministry, he was surrounded by people who wanted to take matters into their own hands. Some wanted to overthrow the government powers that ruled them. Others were determined to keep those underneath them in their place. However, Jesus maintained an entirely different perspective. We call it the Golden Rule, but it's actually the words he spoke to his disciples as recorded in Luke 6:31, "Just as you want men to do to you, do the same to them."

If we put His words in the context of the creative artist, it sounds like this: if you want to get ahead in your career, you have to help others get ahead. If you want people to praise your work, you must praise theirs. If you want your art to make an impact, you must help other artists to make an impact.

There's no joy in success if you have to destroy and diminish others to get it. That kind of life will eventually repel the very people you seek to win over. Make sure that you are finding ways to treat your fellow artists as you wish to be treated, and patiently wait for the time that God chooses to give your art a platform that makes the world take notice.

Prayer

Father, I've often looked around and felt like no one has been noticing my work. I'm tempted to take matters into my hands. But I know that your will is for me to humble myself and exalt others, until the time you choose to exalt me. Help me to treat other artists in my world with respect, honor, and love, so that they will in turn be inspired to treat others the same way. I know you'll get the ultimate glory as I show genuine love for those around me. In Jesus' name, amen.

Scripture To Meditate On

Love must be sincere. Hate what is evil; cling to what is good. Be devoted to one another in love. Honor one another above yourselves.
- Romans 12:9-10

DAY 8

The Power Of A Principle

Uriah, a soldier in David's army, is summoned to the king's palace from the battlefield. he is showered with gifts and praise by the king himself. He is basically commanded to take a vacation and to enjoy a night of passion with his wife, whom he had probably not seen for months. Any weary soldier would have been happy to accept this offer.

Except Uriah didn't take the offer. He felt a moral obligation to his brothers on the battlefield. While he had the right to let his guard down, he knew *having* a right didn't *make* it right. So he slept on a floor outside of the palace on two consecutive nights rather than violate his principles.

The full story is that Uriah was being set up by King David to cover up his affair with Uriah's wife Bathsheba. Eventually, Uriah's desire to do the right thing led to his death, orchestrated by order of the king. (You can read the entire story in 2 Samuel chapters 11 and 12.)

We can learn from Uriah's example as creative artists. There will be times in our careers where we are presented with opportunities that may seem harmless. They may even feel like a blessing. But we can be sure that if an opportunity violates a principle, it's most likely not a good idea. We should never compromise doing what's right in order to do what's comfortable.

In any situation that makes you question your principles, think, pray, and ask God to protect you from any opportunity that isn't truly from him. Even if it hurts in the short term, you'll find that aligning yourself with Godly principles is worth the sacrifice every time.

Prayer

Father, I need your guidance every day when it comes to my decisions on which roads to take and which opportunities to accept. I desire the best for my life, but I know that sometimes what looks good can actually harm me in the long run. Help me to stand strong on the principles of your Word and grant me the wisdom to know when I'm in danger of violating the moral and ethical standards you've established in my heart. In Jesus' name, amen.

Scripture To Meditate On

My son, do not let wisdom and understanding out of your sight, preserve sound judgment and discretion; they will be life for you, an ornament to grace your neck. Then you will go on your way in safety, and your foot will not stumble. - Proverbs. 3:21-2

DAYS 9-11
Visualize Your Goals

ALLEN C. PAUL

DAY 9

Words Matter

Many people use their social media voice as a platform to announce their plans and goals: how they will get healthy, lose weight, find a better job, and find the right spouse. There's one problem, however – it's just words. Very seldom do we find out whether our friends actually followed through with their lofty goals. It's easy to state your intentions publicly , but it's much harder to follow through.

If you want an example of a big announcement, look no further than Joshua. In the midst of battle as leader of the Isrealites, he talked to nature itself and gave an outrageous command. "Sun, stand still over Gibeon, and you, moon, over the Valley of Aijalon." (Joshua 10:12b).

Had we been there, we might have pulled Joshua aside and asked him pointedly, "Have you lost it? You expect God to freeze time? Shouldn't you think twice before making a huge announcement like that? You'll look foolish if it doesn't happen!"

But Joshua's assertion wasn't based on his own power. He was speaking the command of God. Joshua didn't tell the sun what to do. God did. Joshua spoke these words with confidence because he knew, at that moment, God was intervening on his behalf. The announcement was a public declaration of God's authority, rather than an attempt by Joshua to gain personal recognition.

So by all means, promote your plans and announce your goals, but don't do it to impress others. Make statements that reveal your trust in God's power. Set goals that are based on his desires and ability to make them come to pass, and you'll find that your words will take on a power you've never experienced before.

Prayer

Father, I know you have given me amazing opportunities to showcase your power in my life. But I sometimes shrink away from using the words that prove my trust in you. Help me to shake off the fear of speaking confidently about your plans for me, but protect me from setting goals that are self-motivated rather than God-motivated. I want to show the world how amazing you are through my gifts and talents. In Jesus' name, amen.

Scripture To Meditate On

"For my thoughts are not your thoughts, neither are your ways my ways," declares the LORD."As the heavens are higher than the earth, so are My ways higher than your ways and My thoughts than your thoughts. As the rain and the snow come down from heaven, and do not return to it without watering the

earth and making it bud and flourish, so that it yields seed for the sower and bread for the eater, so is My word that goes out from My mouth: It will not return to Me empty, but will accomplish what I desire and achieve the purpose for which I sent it.
- Isaiah 55:8

DAY 10

Promoting Without Pride

Have you ever seen an advertisement for a product that didn't claim to be the best? It's a pretty rare occasion. One famous example is an insurance company that ran a series of ads showing both their own prices and their competitors' – even when their competitors' rates were lower. However, the point of these ads was to win over the customer's trust. By admitting their flaws, this company wanted you to believe they had your best interest at heart. They were still trying to be the best.

When we have to promote ourselves, we often experience a moment of awkwardness. Many of us have been taught not to push ourselves above others, so we cringe when we are told to promote our work. How can we promote our work without appearing prideful?

Jesus provides the example. While he prepared for ministry, he purposely hid himself from public view. But when it was time to share the Kingdom of God, Jesus chose accessible and visible places to spread his message. He went to where the people were and told them to let their light shine. His purpose was not to bring glory to himself, but to give others permission to use their own gifts to glorify God and to bless others.

Letting your light shine, in other words, isn't a selfish act. It's a testimony to others that you serve a good Father, and that they should too. Your artistic excellence and abilities can advertise themselves. As Proverbs 27:2 says, it's best to let someone else praise you, but we should also have a Godly confidence in our craft and in sharing our gift with others. Our ultimate goal is not to put ourselves above everyone else, but rather to offer a glimpse of the Creator, who is above everything.

Prayer

Father, you are the source of all my blessings, and when my work is exalted or promoted, you should get the ultimate credit. Help me to see that my gifts and talents are really just another way to show the world how amazing you are. Give me the proper perspective of promotion, so that as I honor you, you will provide all the connections and visibility I need to succeed.

Scripture To Meditate On

No one from the east or the west or from the desert can exalt themselves. It is God who judges: he brings one down, he exalts another.
– Psalms 75:6

DAY 11

Ready for Anything

"Be careful what you wish for!" You've heard people say this when we desire things without considering the possible problems that accompany our wishes. Those who desire fame may not realize the amount of work and public scrutiny they'll face. Those who desire wealth don't realize how hard it is to keep it, and how it affects their relationships and family connections. Those who wish for success don't often take all the sacrifices necessary into account. However, when God gives us a dream or a vision, we should be ready for anything.

Joseph was a boy who was given a dream of ownership, authority, and purpose. In a way, he didn't wish for these things; they were prophecies that were thrust upon him. Nevertheless, because he chose to accept and to share his dreams, he became a target for murder, deceit, prison, and exile. he truly got much more than he bargained for. Yet, in all that he went through, he never gave up on his dream.

When we set up our dreams and visions for the future, we should expect bumps in the road, obstacles in the way, and detours that will try to take us off of the path to success. These shouldn't be surprises. If God has given you a vision or a goal, he knows what you'll have to overcome to get there. The real test is to be ready for anything on the way to fulfilling your purpose – even the things you've never encountered before. You can rest assured that God has already seen it, and he's ready to get you through it.

Prayer

Father, your Word says that we'll have trouble and tests, and my life is no different. I know I'll face hard times and opposition, even when I'm pursuing the goals that you've placed in my heart. Help me to trust you when it seems like everything is going against the plans you've set out for me, and strengthen me as I work to achieve my dreams and goals. I trust and rely on You in every circumstance, because I know you'll always be with me. In Jesus' name, amen.

Scripture To Meditate On

I have told you these things, so that in me you may have peace. In this world you will have trouble. But take heart! I have overcome the world.
- John 16:33

DAYS 12-14
Invest In Your Craft

DAY 12

Seedtime and Harvest

Some people are gifted at growing plants. Talented gardeners like these are said to have a 'green thumb', but I'm pretty sure that my thumbs are considered a pale shade of yellow. Everything I try to grow that has a stem or a flower is DOA as soon as I turn around. I remember with embarrassment when we bought Chia pets for our children, and even those tiny ceramic heads, which only require a little sprinkle of water and sunlight, failed to produce any greenery for our kitchen. Clearly, God was gracious by not making me a farmer.

My inability to grow things is why I'm fascinated with farming. I'm reminded of this when I see the myriad fruits and vegetables in the produce section of my local grocery store. It's amazing to me that someone works around the clock to make sure each plant makes it from the seed, to maturity as a plant, to harvest and production, and finally to my plate or my kitchen. Do we ever think about how amazing that process is?

As creatives, we're often put in charge of seeds that are just as powerful, but that seem insignificant at the time. Our ideas, creative impulses, and visions are not just Chia pet thoughts. They could grow and help to give millions of people inspiration, encouragement, and happiness. But if we see ourselves as 'brown thumb' creatives, we'll never hang on until the harvest comes.

I'm sure you have had 'brown thumb' thoughts as you've gone through seasons where your creative seeds seem dormant. But God has reminded us that seedtime and harvest never really stops. In Genesis 8:22, he tells Noah, who has endured forty days and nights of things being wiped out, that "seedtime and harvest will not cease." Noah must have thought that he would never see a tree or flower again during those storms. God wanted Noah to remember that the same principles that gave the earth food and vegetation before the flood would be reinstated – and he could count on them.

Remember, God never puts a limit on the harvest. As long as you keep planting your creative ideas in good soil, there will be a blessing on the other end.

Prayer

Father, you have entrusted me with seeds of creativity that can bless others. You knew that my mind, my abilities, and my circumstances presented the right conditions for this seed to grow. Give me the confidence and assurance that, as I nurture the seeds of my creative passions, you will provide the resources to bring them to maturity, and that they will produce fruitful results for myself and for others. Remind me to trust you for everything I need to be a wise and effective creative artist. In Jesus' name, amen.

Scripture To Mediate On

Let us not become weary in doing good, for at the proper time we will reap a harvest if we do not give up.
- Galatians 6:9

DAY 13

Being Smart With God's Resources

It's sad when you think about the list of entertainers who have made millions of dollars over their careers and are now broke and bankrupt. It's a pretty long list. Recently, Michael Jackson's Neverland Ranch was sold to yet another buyer, because it was originally auctioned off to pay for the debts his estate was liable for. Even the King of Pop was not king when it came to financial burdens.

Money and creativity can be a scary combination. Those of us who find our joy in the arts can sometimes be intimidated or scared to handle the business side of things, thinking that it's better to leave money issues to those who are more comfortable with it. But that's not true wisdom. While God has gifted some people with administrative and financial savvy, he has given us all principles that we can use to maintain more balance in our finances. More importantly, God makes it clear that our finances have a big influence on how our lives are directed – which means for artists, it affects how we create.

Think about the stress and worry that fill your mind when there's a financial burden looming. Are you able to create freely in those times? Or is it a struggle? When the Bible states that the borrower is slave to the lender in Proverbs, it's not a stretch to say that the creative's abilities are also chained when there's financial stress. This doesn't mean we can't create when we have other responsibilities, but it does mean that we should avoid unnecessary financial burdens as much as possible.

To overcome the worries of money, we must first acknowledge that God has given us the ability and the principles we need to overcome them. As creatives, we aren't bound to a life of poverty and lack of resources. The principles of being frugal, not getting into debt, and investing God's resources wisely into our creative businesses aren't just good ideas – they are God's way of freeing us to be the creators he designed us to be.

Prayer

Father, you have given me resources and finances both to live, and to use as seed to invest in my creative pursuits. I admit, sometimes I become worried and consumed by the fears of not having enough money to pursue my dreams. But you have given me steps and principles in your Word to help me reach my goals without becoming burdened by money worries. Help me see that you are my ultimate source, and may I become a wiser and more effective manager of the funds you've blessed me with. In Jesus' name, amen.

Scripture To Meditate On

And do not set your heart on what you will eat or drink; do not worry about it. For the pagan world runs after all such things, and your Father knows that you need them. But seek His kingdom, and these things will be given to you as well.

For where your treasure is, there your heart will be also.
- Luke 12:29-31, 34

DAY 14

The True Nature of Giving

Even if you haven't been in church a lot, you've likely heard the phrase, *It's more blessed to give than to receive.* We're accustomed to hearing people repeat that at Christmas time or other moments where we're expected to open our hearts and wallets to a person or cause. What's interesting is that this phrase only appears once in the Bible. Paul mentions it in Acts 20:35 and attributes the words to Jesus. However, it's not recorded in any of the gospels.

This isn't to question the statement's accuracy. I want you to look at the context of that statement and figure out why Paul mentioned it in the first place. When he makes this statement, he is giving a farewell address to a church he has pastored for years. Paul wants them to understand the reasoning behind his ministry, and he makes sure to mention that he worked for a living while he was pastoring.

Watch how Paul connects blessings with his work ethic. "And I have been a constant example of how you can help those in need by working hard. You should remember the words of the Lord Jesus: It is more blessed to give than to receive" (Acts 20:35)

The context is clear – he didn't depend on their charity or his talents to survive. Instead, he worked in what some might call his "9 to 5", so he could provide for himself and for others.

Most artists would agree that working as a creative involves a lot of financial sacrifices. However, it's not always that we see our work as the means by which we can bless others. But that's exactly why Paul continued making tents, despite his gifting as a leader and writer. He knew the purpose of his gift was to minister to others and, while being immensely talented, those talents did not entitle him to be supported by anyone else.

As you work in your creative field, remember you're not supposed to be the only one that benefits from your labors. You've been blessed with abilities in order to help those around you. It's when you give out of a heart of generosity that you experience the blessings that Paul alludes to. As you give, you grow into the fullness of the artist God called you to be.

Prayer

Father, you know I'm constantly trying to excel as an artist, build fulfilling relationships, and increase my financial resources. Yet even as I work hard to achieve my goals, never let me forget that my abilities are meant to help others and not just myself. Point me toward those that my talents and gifts can bless, and help me to see their needs as equal to my own. Help me live out the principle that it is more blessed to give than to receive. In Jesus' name, amen.

Scripture To Mediate On

Sell your possessions and give to charity; make yourselves money belts which do not wear out, an unfailing treasure in heaven, where no thief comes near nor moth destroys. For where your treasure is, there your heart will be also.
- Luke 12:33 (NASB)

DAYS 15-17
Challenge Yourself To Grow

DAY 15

The Importance of Identity

"**I**'m only happy when I'm performing." "I feel alive when I'm creating." "I live to dance/sing/write."

My guess is you've said something like this, or at least you've felt this way at some time. We creatives tend to see our art as a central part of our being. We love our creative activities so much that we can't really imagine life without them. Understandable, yes. But is this a healthy way of looking at ourselves?

Samson, famous strong man of the Bible, is a perfect example of placing too much trust in our gifts. When we first meet him in Judges 13, he is blessed with superhuman strength, is in full possession of his gifts, and is essentially unstoppable. He destroys armies singlehandedly. He avoids capture with ease when his enemies come after him. He's the epitome of self-confidence. But after he submits to Deliah's wooing and allows her to cut his hair, his dependence on his gifts becomes painfully obvious. His confidence and bravado vanishes with his strength, and his lack of connection to God becomes clear. What made him feel special and fulfilled was taken away, and rather than a ruler, he became a slave. He was lowered to the position of begging God to revive his gifts.

Likewise, when we depend on our talents, we risk becoming enslaved by the self-confidence we feel when we're operating in them. Rather than becoming a blessing, it becomes an addictive force that pulls away from a central truth – God loves us as we are, with or without our talents.

It's okay to have a sense of fulfillment while we are using our talents. But we must never let our gifts become the *source* of our fulfillment. Remind yourself today and daily that you are crucified with Christ – your own identity is hidden when you take on Christ's identity. And that leaves no room for an identity based solely on our gifts.

Prayer

Father, you are the true foundation of my identity, and you made me in your image. Still, at times I find myself relying on my talents and gifts to bring me satisfaction. Never let me find my joy and fulfillment only in what I create. Turn my heart to you and help me see myself as a child of God first, and a creative artist second. That way, my gifts will always remain in the proper perspective – as tools that I can use to praise and glorify you. In Jesus' name, amen.

Scripture To Meditate On

I have been crucified with Christ; it is no longer I who live, but Christ lives in me; and the [life] which I now live in the flesh I live by faith in the Son of God, who loved me and gave himself for me.
- Galatians 2:20 (NKJV)

DAY 16

Giving It All Away

What is the one thing you can't live without? Some people might say their spouse. Or their home. Or perhaps their favorite cup of coffee (if they really like coffee). Those who love God would likely say they can't live without him. That's a legitimate claim. But does that mean we're willing to give up everything else but him?

That's a little bit harder. The truth is, we all have a list of things that we feel are necessary for our survival. We know we need food, water, and shelter. But we also have subconsciously created another list – and that list often includes our dreams and desires.

In Mark chapter 12, Jesus is examining the offerings that people are bringing into the temple. He sees many religious leaders, people with resources to spare, giving big sums. He then sees a widow cast in two mites. In our modern currency, her offering would only be worth a few pennies. Many of us know that Jesus commended the widow for giving all her resources away. But what he doesn't mention is how she was going to survive without them. There's no subsequent discussion of how they should help her or an immediate financial blessing that she would experience.

I'm not saying Jesus didn't care about her needs. I'm saying that Jesus fully understood what it meant to give everything away. When he left heaven, he left without any of his heavenly resources. He gave away intimate closeness with the Father. He accepted a role as a human being that was entirely foreign.

As a creative artist, there are times you will be asked to give up everything you have known before and take on a whole new direction – whether it's a new career path, a scary creative project, or something else – and, unless you possess the faith to give everything away, you may miss the opportunity.

God doesn't promise to replace everything we give away, but he does promise to walk with us every step of the way. And that should be enough to give us confidence in every situation.

Prayer

Father, you gave up your son to provide me with salvation. Jesus gave up his position in heaven, and eventually gave his life to save me from my sins. Help me to be willing to give up what I think I can't live without in order to experience a life that is based on faith. I never want to let anything I possess or my current circumstances to distract me from following you wholeheartedly. In Jesus' name, amen.

Scripture To Meditate On

He who finds his life will lose it, and he who loses his life for my sake will find it.

- Matthew 10:39 (NKJV)

ALLEN C. PAUL

DAY 17

Worship Or Work?

Maybe you just got home after a long day of creating, volunteering, or serving. Or perhaps you've completed a huge project that took a lot out of you. You've spent every ounce of your energy using your gifts in their intended purpose. You should feel a sense of accomplishment and fulfillment. But you don't. Instead of happiness, you feel emptiness.

You've heard the cliché that when we do what we love, we're not really working. But the application is often totally inaccurate. There are times when even the things that bring us joy and fulfillment can start to feel like duty instead of privilege. Instead of being energized, we get jaded and frustrated. This is true even when you work in a church setting. No artist is immune to the burden of burnout.

Martha, the sister of Mary and Lazarus, experienced this feeling when she was serving Jesus and his disciples during one of their visits to their home. Martha, by every account, was a willing servant, someone who felt called to be a helpful agent in Jesus' ministry. Yet, in the midst of doing what she was good at, she felt unappreciated and unfulfilled. Her method of blessing others became a burden for her.

You may know what Jesus' response was when Martha requests her sister Mary's assistance, who was at the feet of Jesus hanging on his every word. Jesus lovingly corrects Martha and lets her know that Mary has made a better choice of prioritizing attention on the Savior rather than on her service. Note that Jesus doesn't condemn Martha's work ethic. He simply points out that without the balance of worship, work becomes a burden, even when you are working within your gifting.

Make sure that as you work and serve others with your talent, you never forget the importance of connecting with the One you are serving. God promises to sustain you when you wait on him and stay focused on him, not only as you work for him.

Prayer

Lord, I know that I'm blessed with gifts to provide for my family, bless others, and serve your kingdom. Yet, I also know that working for you only gets me so far. Never let me forget that my greatest fulfillment is found in worshiping you and growing as your child, rather than in proving my worth and value through my accomplishments. Keep me in balance so that my worship and my work always honor you. In Jesus' name, amen.

Scripture To Mediate On

Even youths grow tired and weary, and young men

stumble and fall; but those who hope in the LORD will renew their strength. They will soar on wings like eagles; they will run and not grow weary, they will walk and not be faint.
- Isaiah 40:30-31

DAYS 18-21
Evangelize Through Your Gift

ALLEN C. PAUL

DAY 18

Lights Out

As a creative, you may be one of many artists who find it hard to fall asleep. You may find that as the hours wind down toward midnight, your energy and inspiration actually increase. Some studies have suggested a link between the creative mind and an inability to sleep, as if to say that insomnia is a good thing for the artist.

I believe every person has a unique rhythm to their daily routine, but it's pretty common for musicians and creative artists to have much of their lives dedicated to events that happen at night. For these creative professionals, as the song says, "The night time is the right time."

However, in scripture, night time is often a bad time. Even Jesus warns his disciples about staying in the dark. In John 9:16, he says "I must work the works of him that sent me, while it is day: the night cometh, when no man can work."

Jesus doesn't mean that creatives can't work or create in the nighttime – far from it. Sometimes, we are the only people of the Light who are awake when other believers are asleep. But in the spiritual sense, night time represents the moments when the ability to see God clearly is difficult, and the oppressive spirit of the enemy makes our faith feel small.

It's important for us as artists to be wary about allowing darkness to be a friend. While God will always be present with us, if we're not careful, we can slide into moments of spiritual blindness because we become accustomed to 'night vision'. Not everything we see in the darkness is good for us. Remember, even when you work late into the night, keep God's light in your heart and spirit.

Prayer

Father, you've given us your light to carry into dark places, and your Word tells me to let Your light shine. But I also know that darkness has a way of influencing me when I least expect it. Help me to keep my heart and mind pure and focused on you when I'm in environments and circumstances that seem to mask your presence. Your Word will be a lamp unto my feet and a light unto my path, no matter where my career takes me. In Jesus' name, amen.

Scripture To Meditate On

But you are a chosen people, a royal priesthood, a holy nation, God's special possession, that you may declare the praises of him who called you out of darkness into His wonderful light.
- 1 Peter 2:9

DAY 19

You Are The Gift

Whether it's Christmas time, a birthday party, or some other celebration, there's nothing quite like the moment when someone is presented with a gift. Even the people who know what's in the gift box watch with eager anticipation, waiting to see the gift revealed and the reaction of the recipient. There's something about the process of opening a present that attracts everyone to watch the unveiling.

As a creative, you've probably been accustomed to people referring to your talent or ability as a gift. It is true that you have been given a special talent that you are able to share with others. That's the definition of a gift – something you received from someone else. The problem occurs when we feel people only love us for our gifts.

When we perceive that people only want our gifts, we can become jaded, overly sensitive, or worse, addicted to approval. We could equate it to the child that rips open the package to get to the gift and discards the package without a thought. If we are merely packages that contain the gifts, we can find ourselves questioning our own value.

However, God never emphasizes the gift over the giver. When we are using our gifts to bless others, we're doing more than giving some*thing* away. We are actually giving *ourselves* away.

The time, energy, and discipline to create is a sacrifice you willingly make. When someone reads your poem, hears your song, or watches you perform, they are actually getting a part of you. While your creation is certainly valuable, *you* will always be more valuable than what you create. Why? Because God says you are. When he prepared his ultimate gift for us, he didn't give us a product or a talent. He gave us a person. Nothing could express how valuable we are to him more than his choice to give up everything for our salvation.

Remember as you offer your gifts to others, it's much more than just a creative action. Each time you give creatively, you model Jesus' sacrificial action of giving. Keep in mind how valuable a gift that really is. Without question, it will make a difference.

Prayer

Father, you are the ultimate giver. I thank you for blessing me with everything I need to live a fulfilled life. Now, help me to show that same giving spirit toward the people around me. Remind me that when I pull back from sharing my gifts, I'm actually holding myself back. Lead me and guide me into opportunities to share all I am with others, just as your Son did for me. In Jesus' name, amen.

Scripture To Meditate On

Do nothing out of selfish ambition or vain conceit. Rather, in humility value others above yourselves, not looking to your own interests but each of you to the interests of the others.
- Phillippians 2:3-4

DAY 20

A Time Such As This

As I grow older, I often look back on the days before I became a professional musician. I was still trying to figure this puzzle we call musical performance. All the days spent agonizing over technique, the hours of practicing solo after solo, the nights struggling to create something beautiful – they all seem like a blur now. But at the time, those struggles were all I knew. I assumed that my entire life was about reaching the top, but I had no idea how long it would take me to get there.

Maybe you are in a season of preparing and growing, or perhaps you're already enjoying some of the fruits of your efforts. Either way, you are in the midst of a season that is not over. Your life is moving toward the next chapter whether you like it or not. The question is; are you prepared for what's next?

Esther, the Israelite girl who became a queen, was also once in a season of preparation. She had no idea that the actions she took as a young girl would get her ready to help save her people from a royal decree that would end their legacy. But she was diligent to do all she was asked and, when the time was right, she was prepared to give the right answers and take the right actions.

That's why it's so important to acknowledge that you are really not in charge of your time. Yes, you can set up your daily, weekly, and even your yearly schedule, but the one that ultimately determines what your seasons will look like is God himself. So it only makes sense to ask him what you should be doing now to prepare for what's next. God is the one who will decide the people you will encounter, the challenges you will face, and the blessings that you can one day extend to others.

Each day of this creative journey, remind yourself to take your plans and place them back in his hands. It's only when we give God full access to our lives that he can reveal all the things that we are purposed to accomplish in this life.

Prayer

Father, you've shown me that there's a time for everything. Every occurrence in my life has been allowed and designed by you to make me the person you have destined me to be. Help me, today, to drop anything in my schedule that is not connected to your eternal purpose for me, and help me to recognize the importance of making each day count, for those I love and those I will impact in the future. In Jesus' name, amen.

Scripture To Meditate On

Teach us to number our days, that we may gain a heart

of wisdom.
 - Psalms 90:12

ALLEN C. PAUL

DAY 21

Pressing On

For the last three weeks, you've been digging deeper into your relationship with God and your understanding of creativity. It's my firm belief that by immersing yourself daily in these devotional readings, your faith has grown stronger, your confidence in your calling has increased, and you've developed an ability to see the bigger picture of your creative life. And so the question naturally arises – now what?

Every time you reach the end of a project, complete a major performance or event, or make a major step in your career, that same question sits on your doorstep. And every time, you have a choice, just as you do right now. You could congratulate yourself on finishing and continue doing life as you did before, or you can allow this process to propel you into something more.

Paul knew well the tension between contentment and the pursuit of growth. He often wrote about being content, but he makes it clear that he wasn't settling for his current state. Paul was content physically, but spiritually, he knew there was more to reach for. So it's up to you to take the principles you've studied and meditated on for the last 20 days and turn them into a lifestyle that continues to accelerate your growth and strengthen your trust in God. It's up to you to live the faithful and fulfilled life that God has prepared for you as a creative artist.

The good news? You're not alone. You have a community of artists and creatives that will stand with you and encourage you. Remember to stay connected to The God and Gigs community through Facebook and Twitter and sign up for our newsletter at GodandGigs.com/signup. You can always connect with other faith-focused artists in your area to form accountability groups using the God and Gigs Book and Study Guide. I also welcome your direct emails at allenpaul@godandgigs.com if you'd like to share your journey with me.

Keep growing, keep creating, and, most importantly, keep your connection with God first and foremost in your life.

Prayer

Father, over the last 21 days, you've reminded me that you have a special purpose for me as a creative artist. While I've learned much, there is so much more room to grow. Help me remain humble and teachable no matter how my creative career grows, and remind me that by staying in your Word and connecting with other creatives who follow you, I can find answers in every struggle and circumstance. Keep me in your perfect will, and allow my creative efforts to point more people toward you. In Jesus' name, amen.

Scripture To Meditate On

Brothers and sisters, I do not consider myself yet to have taken hold of it. But one thing I do: Forgetting what is behind and straining toward what is ahead – I press on toward the goal to win the prize for which God has called me heavenward in Christ Jesus.
– Philippians 3:13

Additional Resources from God and Gigs

Books and E-books

God and Gigs: Succeed as a Musician without Sacrificing your Faith

The God and Gigs Study Guide

Available at GodandGigsBook.com and all online bookstores

Breakthrough the Block: 5 Steps to Renewing your Inspiration

Available at Amazon.com and all online bookstores

Audio Resources

The God and Gigs Show Podcast: Subscribe at GodandGigs.com/subscribe-to-podcast

Email Newsletter

Subscribe to the newsletter at
GodandGigs.com/signup

Visit **GodandGigs.com** for information on our local artist events, speaking and consulting services.

www.ingramcontent.com/pod-product-compliance
Lightning Source LLC
Chambersburg PA
CBHW030457010526
44118CB00011B/987